Poetry Matters

Contents

continues over

The United Kingdom Literacy Association

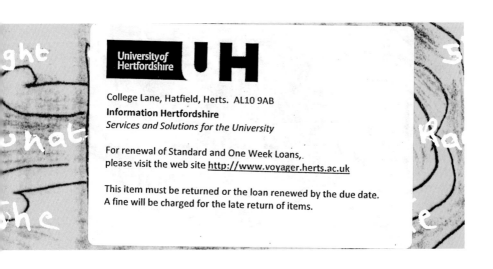

Poetry Matters

By Andrew Lambirth

Minibook 25

UKLA Minibook Series

Series Editor	Eve Bearne
Past series editors	Alison B. Littlefair, Bobbie Neate, Ros Fisher, Susan Ellis

Published minibooks

Genres in the Classroom	Alison B. Littlefair
Running Family Reading Groups	Sue Beverton, Ann Stuart, Morag Hunter-Carsch and Cecelia Oberist
Teaching Handwriting	Peter Smith
Teaching Spelling	Brigid Smith
Supporting Struggling Readers	Diana Bentley and Dee Reid
Phonological Awareness	Frances James
Exploring the Writing of Genres	Beverley Derewianka
The Power of Words	Norma Mudd
Reading to Find Out	Helen Arnold
Moving Towards Literacy with Environmental Print	Linda Miller
Guided Reading	Jo Makgill
English as an Additional Language	Constant Leung
Developing Writing 7 - 13	Roy Corden
Children's Writing Journals	Lynda Graham and Annette Johnson
Tell Me Another... Speaking, Listening and Learning Through Storytelling	Jacqueline Harrett
Drama: Reading, Writing and Speaking Our Way Forward	Teresa Grainger and Angela Pickard
Literature Circles: Better Talking, More Ideas	Carole King and Jane Briggs
Making Reading *Mean*	Vivienne Smith
Storyline: Promoting Language Across the Curriculum	Steve Bell and Sallie Harkness
Miscue Analysis in the Classroom (revised edition)	Robin Campbell
Classroom Action Research in Literacy: a Guide to Practice	Eve Bearne, Lynda Graham and Jackie Marsh
Active Encounters: Inspiring young readers and writers of non-fiction 4-11	Margaret Mallet

Issue number 25: **Poetry Matters** by Andrew Lambirth

Published 2007
ISBN 978 1 897638 40 8

UKLA is willing to allow UKLA members to make multiple copies of up to 10% of this work for distribution within an educational institution or a local authority. Permission need not be sought for such copying.

Published by U<LA
United Kingdom Literacy Association
Attenborough Building, University of Leicester,
University Road, Leicester LE1 7RH, England
www.ukla.org

The United Kingdom Reading Association (UKRA) became the United Kingdom Literacy Association (UKLA) on May 25th 2003.
© *United Kingdom Literacy Association*

Chapter 1

Introduction: poetry matters?

Poetry matters every day. The essence of poetry, its heart, its pulse seems to follow us around everywhere we go. We can be seen tapping out its rhythms with feet, fingers, pens and pencils everyday. When we play with words in jest, love or spite we use the tools and techniques that poets through the ages have utilised to make their "verbal music".

It is in no way exclusive and in every way inclusive. We can hear it everywhere we go, including: the football terraces, the playground, the church, the mosque, the building site, the university and the primary school. It is there in many parts of our day: before bed, in bed, breakfast time, work time and play time. In truth, it is difficult to think of a time or a place when words are never used in special ways; when we do not play with words and their meanings, or create rhyme or verse, or carefully put words together in an order that sounds right and heightens our meaning making. We hear it in many guises including pop song, opera, joke, chant, jingle, sonnet, rap, nursery rhyme and so on. Some we love and are moved by in the deepest ways, others we want to curse and call shallow and dull, but always there is an effect. All of these forms belong to a family called poetry.

Poetry and playfulness

Playing with language to enhance our meaning making comes early. Children enjoy doing this whenever they are together. It prompts laughter and tears and is a powerful part of our communicating repertoires. The point here is that right from the start of our linguistic histories we understand how to enhance the meanings we wish to make. Young children appreciate this kind of language when they hear it. Primary school teachers soon become aware of the influential characters in their class by the power of their ludic use of language. Poetry, as it has been written through history, also 'plays' with words and structures and manipulates them to enhance meanings, sometimes, in the most profound ways. This is the pinnacle of this early play with language and suggests that it is crucial to build on the early enjoyment of the manipulation of words for effect. David Crystal (1998) contends that it is healthy and 'normal to be (linguistically) abnormal by engaging in language play' (Crystal, 1998:58).

Children and Poetry

Children use rhyme and verse to skip, clap and dance to. Their movement to the beat of this verse is intrinsic to their play and their enjoyment of this form of language. They seem to share with some of the world's poets, past and present, the pleasure of the 'taste' and tingle of delicious and strange sensations of words on their tongues and the effect of rhythm on their bodies. With so much implicit understanding of this world of verse and rhyme, the potential to build upon these foundations looks limitless.

Poetry and rhyme is so inclusive that it seems that we sometimes fail to recognise it when we hear it and miss how fundamental it is to our every day experience of the world. It is important to remind ourselves of our understanding and ability to utilise its techniques.

Anxieties

If poetry and rhyme is part of our everyday experience it does seem strange that the area of literature called 'poetry' often causes so much uneasiness in adults when they are asked to read, write or discuss it. Poetry seems to be the most neglected form of literature in terms of adult readership. These days, primary school teachers will know the popularity in their classrooms of poetry written for children, but this enthusiasm for verse seems to be extinguished later in life. So, something must happen - could it be schools and the nature of the approach to poetry in these institutions?

This book invites teachers to reflect upon their own knowledge of poetry and rhyme and then ask children to do so as well. When we recognise its fundamental inclusion in our own experience, we can go on to examine the work of others who have learned how to explicitly utilise it for different purposes and audiences. It is hoped that building on these foundations, teachers and children will feel more confident to enjoy poetry and be convinced of its potential as one of the most important, profound and powerful means of communication between individuals.

Poetry for learning

The benefits of using poetry in the classroom are astounding. It may be useful here to remind us of some of them. Firstly, its ability to generate delight means it is a great motivator for encouraging reading. It has the capability of changing children's fundamental attitudes to reading by drawing on their interest in word play. The wealth of verse published by our modern poets seems to be able to tap into children's humour and experience of life at their level. Children adore the work of Michael Rosen, Brian Patten and Roger McGough, to name but three, and will want to hear it again and again. Secondly, research informs us (Bryant and Bradley, 1985) that children who are exposed to rhyme and alliteration from an early age develop a greater phonological awareness, contributing directly to the learning of strategies readers need to employ. In addition to this, we know that poetry encourages concentration and listening skills; it also helps develop literal and inferential comprehension and response. The writing of poetry, with its emphasis on vocabulary and heightened language use can only help develop the writer's ability to experiment with the potency of written forms. Children who are encouraged to write poetry also become involved in a process of self-discovery – it assists children in understanding their experiences of everyday life.

This book

The book will first of all tackle the question of 'what is poetry?' It will go on to discuss how to create a classroom ready to interest and excite children with this form of writing. It will look at ways to plan teaching to immerse children in poetry and encourage them to write it for themselves.

The aim of this book is to give primary school teachers the confidence and conviction to use and enjoy poetry in their classrooms. The book is written to provide the background and the ideas to do this successfully, while not forgetting that the teacher's personal pleasure in poetry, in whatever form s/he chooses to enjoy it, will energise the teaching within the classroom.

Chapter 2

Inner debates - coming to terms with poetry

The problem is
There are too many poetry experts....
But poetry experts make it their business to tell you
What kind of poems you should like,
Not me,
I know what I like

Benjamin Zephaniah (1997:1)

This section looks at what primary teachers need to know about poetry to enjoy it and teach it effectively. It begins with the question: 'What is poetry?' This may seem a rather strange question to start with; after all, the National Curriculum (DfEE, 1999) is clear that poetry is a defined form of writing and will be part of the range of literature that is offered in classrooms.

Everyone knows what a poem is... don't they?

However, leafing through just one of the huge choice of anthologies of poetry available to children, it soon becomes clear that the boundaries between poetry and other forms of writing, even other forms of art are rather blurred. An example of this is the 'poem' 'The Honey Pot' by Alan Riddell that can be found in *The Kingfisher Book of Children's Poetry* edited by Michael Rosen (1985). It consists of a 'swarm' of lower case letter bs, which appear to be gathering around an unseen object.

Why should this be classified as poetry?

- It could be perceived as more of a pictorial representation than one made from words, yet it does have letters in it.

- Can we read it? Well, it depends on which way we take 'read' to mean. Do we need to 'read' it like we may 'read' a picture?
- Like other poems, we do puzzle over it and like other poems we can discuss it and reach our own individual conclusions about it.
- It certainly plays with language and invites readers to approach the challenge it playfully sets.
- Of course, it is in a poetry book, so that might make it poetry.

Which ever way we look at it, whether we like it, love it or loath it, this is just one example of work classified as poetry by a writer or publisher that does not adhere to traditional forms we are familiar with. In all areas of the art world: painting, music and dance, there are those who present work that challenges traditional conceptions of that particular art form and highlights the subjective nature of the values we hold in aesthetics. When teachers are asked to 'teach poetry', a seemingly simple instruction becomes rather problematic, and not at all straightforward. This, by the way, could be one reason why many teachers are apprehensive when approaching poetry in their classrooms.

Benjamin Zephaniah's statement 'I know what I like' foregrounds an individual's empowerment to make their own values and come to their own conclusions about art and in this case poetry. The traditional 'experts' in the academies of art and poetry, who in the past provided institutionalised definitions and even interpreted poems for their readers have also had their views questioned and labelled as 'subjective' rather than 'objective' and scientific – we no longer have to take their values as truths. Art and poetry exist within the eye of the beholder whether we like it or not!

This may sound all very democratic and egalitarian, but where does it leave the teachers who are required by law to teach poetry? If we conclude that definitions of poetry lie in an individual reader, then it makes sense for teachers to reflect upon what they 'like' and understand as being poetry at its best and make this a priority. Dunn et al. describe this form of reflection as an 'inner debate': 'A teacher's inner debate about what poetry is will certainly be worthwhile and should improve her teaching. This is whether she comes to a fixed and satisfying definition or not (Dunn, Styles & Warburton, 1987:34).

Teaching poetry is exciting and stimulating when teachers draw on their own understanding of it. The debate that teachers have with themselves will power the teaching in the class. This understanding will come after self immersion in a range of different kinds of poetry, picking out the forms and styles and the subjects that interest and move them in some way.

Here is a checklist of activities for teachers wanting to reassess their own understanding and experience of poetry:

- Reflect upon the verse you enjoy already; this will include your favourite love songs, rock songs, poems from your childhood, rhymes you sing to your own children at night, jokes you have heard, poems you know and love from the literary 'tradition' and so on.
- Find a time in your week when you can read poetry aloud.
- Read anthologies compiled for children and adults.
- Pick out your favourite poets and read more of their work.
- Have faith in your own intuitive response.
- Listen to a range of poems for children and adults read by experienced poetry readers on tapes and CD. This way you will hear the musical dimension of poetry.
- Listen to the songs, rhymes and verses children are using in the playground and the street.

Watch the responses of the children you read poems to - which ones do they enjoy and what is it about them which makes them so delicious?

Common features of poetry

Having established that poetry can come in all shapes and sizes and forms we need to look at some common features.

Language

Poetry has been said to use words in special ways. It takes the language we use every day and makes it strange; it defamiliarizes it for us. Shklovsky (1973) made an analogy with walking and dancing; we walk everyday and as a result we cease to be aware of doing it. Poetry does for language what dance does to walking - it transforms the mundane into the surprising, the new and the enlightening: 'A dance is a walk which is felt, even more accurately, it is a walk constructed to be felt' (Shklovsky , cited in Jefferson and Robey, 1986:19).

Poetry has also been said to use words with the greatest possible precision and evocativeness. Here, poetry's power lies in its economical use of words, while still making succinct meanings that have enormous penetrative force – the words do not just inform, as in other kinds of writing, but can inflame (Scannell, 1987).

Poetry's Effect

It was James Britton who described poetry as an experience: 'a carefully organised, structured experience' (1958). W.H. Auden and John Garret described poetry as memorable speech (1935). Poetry achieves its effects by its unique devices: its rhythm, rhyme, its repetitions and so on, causing readers to be moved emotionally and excited intellectually. It is this novel experience, caused by these poetic devices that set it apart from other forms of literature.

Each poem has its own individuality, something that will draw the reader to it. This is sometimes described as its 'heart' – often its main idea, some kind of focal point that ignites the poem's effect and the experience it produces.

Poetry's rhythmic, patterned nature

Poetry can look unique on the page. Its shape and form can sometimes appear very different to prose. In addition to this, the shape and form can contribute to its meaning. Shape or concrete poems do this very blatantly, but other forms of poetry can achieve this in much more subtle ways. The structure of the poem, its length of line and syllabic make-up of the words forms the rhythm of the piece. For example, the rhythm can be jaunty and light or it can be slow and drawn out and in many cases can add mood and atmosphere, enriching the meaning and the general effect the poet wants to create. For example, Ted Hughes' 'Esther's Tomcat' given in Benton and Benton (1989), uses very 'hard' sounding words, utilising rather flat and very short vowels. This may be a deliberate device linked directly to the subject of this poem, which is a rough, tough tomcat. For this reader, it conjures up a 'no nonsense', 'knows what he wants', 'no messing about' character, who has had to be this practical and straight in order to survive. This is not the kind of cat to be stroked and loved by any fireside. It is these 'sound effects', created by carefully chosen words, which add to the meaning of the piece, making the reader look at the cat in this way.

How to read and respond to a poem

"'Poetry gives most pleasure', said Coleridge, 'when only generally and not perfectly understood'; and perfect understanding will sometimes extinguish pleasure"
(A. E. Houseman, 1933 cited in D. Crystal (ed),1998)

When we respond to a poem we often do so without thinking. We may join in the recital, laugh, and sometimes, cry. There will also be times when we respond inwardly, quietly, aesthetically, and at these times we may be unable to put into words just what the experience is like:

> Perhaps aesthetic experience is even better typified by the gaps between 'the ordinary spectator's phrases; by the wordless moments when the spectator is poised in the act of simply apprehending… rather than remarking…' Most of the comments or remarks indicative of the experience are retrospective in that they are about it rather than part of it.
> (Collinson, 1985: 271 cited in Benton, 2000)

Collinson is writing about viewing a painting, but this aesthetic response must be the same in many ways as when we read a poem. This quiet moment, may be the highest form of response where our own verbalisation of the experience can not express the feeling invoked. When we introduce children to poems, we need to attempt to share and compare our reading experience, taking everybody's contribution as interesting and valid. By voicing the feelings and effects that the poem creates, children should begin to 'internalise' these responses, adding their own unique strategies, ready for when they read poetry for themselves. Therefore, as teachers, we need to find the words and the framework to discuss our reading of a poem and pass this on to children. The following advice is based upon the suggestions made by Benton and Benton (1989).

When approaching a poem we need to:
1) **respond individually**
2) **respond with the sight**
3) **respond to the sound**
4) **respond to what is unique.**

1. Responding individually

This may include the following:

- Do I like it?
- What do I like about it?
- Are there any comparisons with my own life and the poem's subject?
- How do I find the mood of the poem? Does the mood change by the end of the poem? Do I find it funny? Do I find it sad? How does it make me feel?

The emphasis here is on the importance and validity of an individual response, based upon who we are.

2. Responding with sight

Here, we may focus on:

- How is the poem presented on the page? Look at it as a whole thing as we might a painting.
- Are there any patterns in the language used?
- How long are the lines?
- How are the words spaced out in the line?
- Do any of the words rhyme?
- Is the poem in verses or sections?
- What are its unusual features in terms of layout?

3. Responding to sound

When you read the poem aloud listen and think about what appeals to you. Listen for:

- The sound of the words
- The rhythm of the lines
- The pace of the delivery
- The music of the poetry.

4. Responding to what is unique

When you have read the poem aloud to yourself you may want to look for a central theme, feeling, idea or focal point that strikes you as special. The poem may concentrate on a certain feeling of a certain person at a certain time. It may describe someone or something well. Words may crackle and fizz within poems. Perhaps the mood of the poem is its most remarkable feature.

Responding to poetry as a person will take practice of reading a variety of poems by different poets. It is an enjoyable and uplifting experience. Remember, there can be no definitive or 'correct' interpretation of the poem; equally no one's opinion can be 'wrong'. This means, discussions about poetry are 'safe', non-threatening activities. In the past the study of poetry seemed akin to an I.Q. test or a competition to find the 'right' meaning of a particular poem as though a poem could have a solution in the same way a nut has a kernel (Jacobs, 2001) - once we have cracked it and scooped out the insides, the 'job of work' is complete.

Many commentaries written about poetry often use forms of language that are robust, self-assured and rather pompous. These writers can seem to intellectually bully the reader into agreement through providing what sounds like an objective description of the meaning - as if there could be no other interpretation, implying readers are foolish if they do not agree. To the experienced reader of poetry and criticism this way of addressing an audience may well be challenging and stimulating, but for those who are new to this area of literature and the discourse that surrounds it, they may indeed find it rather dispiriting and threatening. Commentary of this nature is totally inappropriate in the context of early learning environments. A good commentary around a poem will put subjectivity first. Whilst it is possible to describe the shape or form of the poetry - its verses, patterns of rhyming words etc. - when it comes to the meaning and the feelings poetry invoke, then the commentary must own up to its subjectivity, offering views as opinions not facts.

Try going back to a poem that you were made to read at school and rediscover its power by responding as a person rather than as an exam candidate; you may be surprised!

Now that we have come to terms with the multiple dimensions of poetry; we have considered some of its common features and thought about how we can respond to it; the next section will focus upon preparing the environment for poetry within the classroom, one that reflects our own understanding of it and our enthusiasm and commitment to teaching and enjoying poetry.

Chapter 3

Preparing for poetry

Before we think about finding a place for poetry in plans for literacy, it is time to consider making the classroom fit for poetry readers and writers.

Resources

The books

Every classroom should have at the very least six good poetry books in the book area, including picture books at both key stages. These books are the permanent poetry residents of the classroom. They have earned their place because they can offer children a range of quality poems by a range of poets, reflecting the teacher's enthusiasms and poetry's multiple definitions. Before the advent of the renewed Primary National Strategy for literacy, there were specific types of poetry that the National Literacy Strategy (1998) recommended that teachers should teach. Lists like these can be restrictive and suggest a closure over the possibilities of what poetry can be. However, it was not a bad list and one that might help teachers decide what they want to cover. In many schools these were made available in the school for teachers to use as and when they decide to focus on a particular type. Here is the checklist:

Age 3 - 5
Nursery and modern rhymes, chants, action verses, poetry with pre dictable structures and patterned language.

Age 5 - 7
Rhymes with predictable and repeating patterns, poems with similar themes, including poems from a range of cultures, poems by significant children's poets, texts with language play, e.g. riddles, tongue twisters, humorous verse.

Age 7 - 11

Poems based on observation and the senses, shape poems, oral and performance poetry from different cultures, humorous poetry and poems that play with language, word puzzles, puns and riddles, poems based on common themes, classic and modern poetry, range of poetry in different forms, e.g. haiku, cinquain, couplets, lists, thin poems, alphabets, conversations, monologues, syllabics, prayers, epitaphs, songs, rhyming forms and free verse, poems written in other forms (adverts, letter, diary entries, conversations), nonsense verse.

Schools should also stock the poetry that teachers in the school love to read and teach with, so schools should not get stuck on only the range suggested by curriculum documents. Good anthologies will have many of these forms of poetry in them anyway, but teachers and language co-ordinators will need to ensure they have these specific types when planning to immerse the children in these types of poetry over a block of planned work. The next chapter discusses how this might be done.

Listening areas

In all key stages it is important for children to hear poems read by a range of different readers, including poets and actors. Poems should be part of the taped collection of texts available for children to listen to individually or with their friends, using multiple headphones. Children will naturally imitate the reading styles and 'tunes' of their favourite readers. The teacher and the children should be included as poetry readers available on the tapes. These recordings allow the children to hear the magic of the 'verbal music' offered.

Class anthologies

Make a class anthology with the children. Ask the children to choose their favourite poems - perhaps by theme. These books can be illustrated, hand-written, word processed, even illuminated. It might be a big book or a miniature book. Perhaps the children have written a short explanation of why they chose the poem to go along side the entry. Keep the anthologies in the book area to be read anytime.

Poetry routines

Reading times

Every class, regardless of children's age, needs a time in the day for them to browse the collections of books available. To help prevent these times becoming too routine and predictable, add some variety:

- Do a book spread of the poetry books. Scatter the poetry books on the tables and ask the class to walk around them. Ask them to: pick up a book whose cover they find appealing, then show it to the person standing near; find a poetry book that has funny poems in it, share that with their partner; pick up a book that has a poem they like in it, again, share it with someone and so on. The session can end with the children sitting down with a partner to enjoy a poetry book together.
- Have a 'poetry only' day; a reading time when the children can only read poetry, or verse.
- Set out the classroom with 'Book Type Tables'. Each table will have a certain kind of writing on it - fairy tales, comics, non-fiction and poetry. The children choose what they wish to read, or the teacher may encourage certain children to sit with a particular kind of text. The range of text available is made explicit and ensures children have a 'taste' of each one.
- At the end of reading time ask some of the children to read out a 'juicy bit' (Lambirth, 1997) from the book they have been reading. There is nothing quite as juicy as a good poem!

Poet/poem of the week

Ask the children to select a poem of the week.

- Reproduce it as an enlarged text and display it in the classroom, perhaps on the interactive whiteboard.
- Read it regularly, perhaps with the help of the class.
- Encourage the children to read it aloud to the class, alone or as a group. This allows children to see how individuals can put their own voice to the piece. The chosen poem will soon become an 'old friend' that the children will meet again throughout school and, hopefully, their lives.
- Leave Post-it™ labels by the poem for the children to comment on and stick up alongside the displayed poem. They can do this with their own compositions too.

13

Learning and performing

- Learning simple poems by heart can be fun. Poems with a strong rhythm and rhyme attach themselves to children's hearts and mouths with ease.
- Performing poems helps children implicitly understand the uniqueness of this kind of writing – its rhythms, rhymes and structures. Try asking them to convert one form of poetry into another; for example converting a nursery rhyme into a rap, or a rap into a plain chant and so on.

Personal 'Greatest Hits' anthologies

Ask the children to make a personal book of favourite poems, songs, chants and rhymes. These can be professionally published poems or compositions by themselves or their friends. Do this in reading time or independent work periods in literacy sessions.

Poetry is a leisure time activity - read it for pleasure

There will be regular times when teachers will read poetry in shared times within the literacy lesson, teaching and modelling enjoying and appreciating poetry. Here, specific learning objectives are attached to them, but pleasure and excitement should remain at a premium. Children need to perceive poetry as fun and a means to satisfying relaxation. Classroom activities need to reflect this and poetry should be read with this in mind.

Young children can be encouraged to join in with readings of poetry where appropriate - finishing off lines themselves, clapping and singing along, feeling free to comment and respond in any way they wish - all for the pleasure of it.

Older children also need to hear poems read by a teacher who likes reading poems and shows personal interest and enthusiasm in particular poems by particular poets. Poetry is a leisure-time activity and should be promoted and modelled as such. If young people see poetry attached to hard graft and difficult analysis, they will see no reason to incorporate it into their leisure time. Poetry is up against stiff opposition here, but can win through.

Bring back the rope!

Reintroduce the skipping rope into the playground. Where there is a skipping rope there will be skipping rhymes and songs. This is one of the last bastions of the oral tradition, listen to how the rhymes change as they move from lips to lips and from school to school. What a wonderful way for children to begin to understand the essential pulse of poetry!

Orientating children to poetry

The Introduction discussed how teachers could find a place for themselves in poetry. Children also need to feel included and part of the world of poetry. To achieve this, as with all new topics, teachers need to begin with what the children know already. Here are some ideas:

- Ask the children to recall all the poems and rhymes they know by heart. Start with the skipping and clapping rhymes they use in the playground. Space needs to be provided for the inevitable actions involved in the recitation. There may also be arguments over authenticity of the words! Football chants, pop songs, nursery rhymes and advertising jingles will also be offered and shared. They need to be received with enthusiasm and an open-mind - subversive rhymes can be some of the best!
- The children should start work on constructing an anthology of these poems, songs, chants and rhymes. When completed put the book in the reading area, it will become a very popular read. Fig. 1 is an example of a year 4 child's transcribed version of a rhyme she has been reciting orally with her friends outside the classroom.
- Organise a performance of these verses for an assembly. Using the skipping ropes in the assembly, allow them to recite their rhymes. This will celebrate what they know about poems and rhymes.
- Introduce some of the more subversive verse from modern collections of poems written for children.

> I know a little Dutch girl called i shoe sellarea
> and all the boys in the foot ball pitch
> said I shoe sellarea How is your, mother All
> right died in the fish shop last night
> whatwasShe eating Raw fish How did
> She end up like this

Figure 1 'I know a little Dutch girl' transcription of a playground rhyme

With the background pulse of poetry in place, teachers can begin to think about how to effectively plan for making poetry central in the teaching of literacy. The next section looks at this in detail.

Chapter 4

Planning for poetry

The previous section described how teachers could create an 'on-going' environment for reading poetry. This section will discuss ways to plan effectively for the teaching of poetry.

Teaching poetry within the Primary National Literacy Strategy

Since 1998 most schools in England have been using the National Literacy Strategy (NLS,1998) as a framework for planning. From 2006 the renewed Primary National Strategy for literacy has been introduced to effectively replace the old NLS documents. Arguably, a good case was made over the years for the destructive influence of the atomisation of learning objectives on teachers' professional autonomy and creativity and on pupils' learning. Research had discovered (Frater, 2000) that in the most successful schools the National Literacy Framework (1998) had not been followed in literal or fragmented ways, but had been approached as more of a checklist for coverage of the National Curriculum, rather than a blue-print. It was seen as a basis for planning. In successful schools, there was less preoccupation with literal coverage of the termly content of the framework and the teaching of text, sentence and word level objectives had been integrated into a holistic language experience. This is what the renewed Primary National Strategy for literacy potentially offers teachers.

Text, sentence and word level objectives have been dissolved into twelve strands: speaking; listening and responding; group discussion and interaction; drama; word recognition; word structure and spelling; understanding and interpreting texts; engagement with and response to texts; creating and shaping texts; text structure and organisation; sentence structure, punctuation; presentation. The potential for the use of poetry here is enormous and this needs to be celebrated.

Teachers beware!

There seems to be a current trend in some economically advanced English speaking countries to promote a single method of teaching reading which focuses on synthetic phonics. This is advocated in the Primary National Strategy in England, influenced by the Rose Review (DfES 2006a). The Rose Review, commissioned by the United Kingdom's New Labour Government, is described as an 'independent' review of the teaching of early reading. In this document the author recommends the use of synthetic phonics as the principal first strategy for early reading. In the United States of America the National Reading Panel's report (2000) had similar recommendations and in Australia the consultation paper The Victorian Curriculum and Assessment Authority (2004) emphasised the importance of teachers concentrating on basic skills in English teaching to ensure Australia's economic growth.

In my view, teachers need to be wary of this kind of approach to early reading. This could potentially impact detrimentally on the use of poetry with very young children. As I have mentioned, there is much to be celebrated about the revised Literacy Strategy in England yet there appear to have been theoretically contradictory positions contributing to this document. On the one hand it offers the possibilities of more integrated and creative learning, but only *after* very young children have been subjected to fast-paced gruelling repetitive direct instruction. As a response to the Rose Review (2006) the Primary National Strategy for literacy teaching advocates that the teaching of phonics should be introduced as the principal first method for reading to children as young as 4. The Primary National Strategy supports the Rose Review which advocates 'fidelity' (DfES 2006:21) to commercial schemes and packages that teach phonic strategies exclusively, discretely and systematically. There is an enormous amount of research (Bryant and Bradley 1985, Goswami and East, 2000) that describes the importance of poetry and rhyme for beginner readers' phonological understanding. My concern is that hearing good quality poetry read aloud regularly throughout the early years of schooling will not form part of early reading instruction, particularly where teaching relies on discrete and systematically taught phonics schemes. This would be counterproductive as poetry offers language and its sounds in whole words and in a real context. The 'system' for learning to read that the Primary Strategy offers - 'learning to read' and then 'reading to learn' - comes from, in my opinion, a simplistic and false notion of a linear progression of learning (DfES 2006a). It offers a misleading message that children first need to learn how to decode before benefiting from their response to rich texts written for their enjoyment and listening pleasure (DfES 2006b). Indeed, the logic of this position runs counter to early home experiences of children's use of song and rhyme. Hearing a large volume of poetry from a young age greatly helps the process of becoming a reader. Significant early experiences of hearing poetry and rhyme read must never be denied to young children in school. Any approach that does this deserves to be disdainfully rejected by teachers.

Having got that off my chest I want to move on to planning. The unit of work model is championed by the renewed Primary Strategy. The units that are suggested on their web site are now longer in duration and potentially offer teachers greater scope to provide children with a rich poetry experience. With this in mind, teachers may wish to work like this:

1. Teachers decide what needs to be taught within a half term - for example, riddles, tongue twisters and humorous verse. Decide how much time is needed to effectively teach this kind of poetry, perhaps three weeks.
2. Accumulate good quality examples of this kind of poetry from the classroom collection, from the school library, from other teachers' classrooms (with their permission!), Local Authority teacher resource libraries and so on. Make a display of these poems as one way to promote them.
3. Decide on a piece of work that will appropriately conclude this experience with poetry. It may be a tape of children reciting poems, an anthology, and children's own work and so on.
4. In a three-week block, allow the first week or so of literacy lessons for immersion in that particular form of poetry. The emphasis is on the reading, performing, discussing and sharing of ideas. In this half of the block the teacher is concerned to encourage enjoyment of the poems and to point out their key features. Children will be involved in activities that encourage this kind of immersion in shared, guided and independent times.
5. The second half of the block has a composing and/or writing slant and explicitly works towards the completion of the assignment that has been previously set. Shared and guided writing can be important ways of modelling the writing process.

6. Utilise extended writing periods for children to work on writing and publication of their own poems.
7. Poetry can of course be used in cross-curricular planning. Its subjects are numerous and offer rich insights into places, events and experiences. A unit of work like this can be planned to run alongside or within projects and themes being explored in other areas of the curriculum.

Immersion activities

To enjoy and understand poems of particular types, children will need plenty of exposure to them in a variety of interesting ways. Much of this immersion can be carried out in some of the routines for reading poetry discussed in the previous chapter. For very young children immersion activities will be central to the planning and an end in themselves. Children are encouraged to share the experience of reading poetry, comparing responses, discussing opinions, joining in the reading, clapping along and moving to its beat.

Supporting children to go on to write poems means explicitly encouraging them to 'read as writers' (Barrs, 2000). Children can then see themselves as poets, discussing how other poets have achieved the effects they make and then having a go themselves. The Shared Reading time of a literacy lesson provides an excellent opportunity.

Immersion involves:
- Listening to poetry in a range of contexts: on tape, in the playground; in reading times; in shared reading/writing; and in the listening area with friends.
- Speaking: one important form of response is speaking poetry, performing it to others, the creative and expressive performance reflecting the speaker's interpretation of the poem. Speaking will also help children become familiar with the rhythms, images and cadences and this in turn helps their own writing of poetry.
- Conferencing: children will enjoy talking about poetry and they will need to be encouraged to respond to poems intuitively with others in pairs or groups.

- Reading: asking children to listen and read poetry helps the development of essential skills for reading as has been said earlier. But poetry is not there to be just used in this way. Reading poetry is fun and this fun will help reading. So it needs to be read in all elements of a school day and enjoyed.
- Memorising: children know many rhymes off by heart, the teacher can add to these by asking children to memorise poetry deriving from other sources. This should not be a chore as many poems attach themselves to memory so easily because of the rhythms and rhymes.

Introducing a poem

These activities are great in shared time, or need to be modelled with the whole class before being used for independent times.

Titles
Many poems have intriguing titles and these can be a great start to a discussion about the poem. Ask the children to guess what the poem will be about from the title. Conversely read the poem and ask the children to guess the title.

Debate
Issues for debate will include:
- Picturing: comparing what the words in the poem make us see in our 'mind's eye'. A useful question to ask children is 'Where were you when I was reading the poem?' Other questions might include asking about how the children 'saw' people or things in the poem. As well as there being a 'mind's eye' there is also a 'mind's ear' and a 'mind's nose'; can the children 'smell' or 'hear' anything during the reading?
- Connecting: debating the connections children make with what or who is in the poem. This means comparing the children's own lives or experiences with those in the poem.
- Evaluating: what do the children think of the poem and why? An evaluation will involve reasons for the children's conclusions.
- Awareness of language and structures: what do the children notice about patterns within the poem, interesting, puzzling, remarkable words in the poem.

Debate will centre on reader interaction with poetry as referred to in earlier sections.

Interviews

After reading a poem that is rich enough that it can generate these kinds of discussions, ask the children, in pairs, to fold a piece of paper twice and then open it up again. The paper will have four rectangles. Ask the children to formulate four questions that they wish to ask about this poem. It may be a question of the poet about reasons for writing the poem; it could be a question about words that have been used, events or atmosphere. Once the questions have been written down, one in each box, ask the children to move to another pair and read their questions to them. The other pair attempts to answer the questions, and then asks theirs. The answers are written down and then the pairs move on to other children. Questions and answers are then shared in a plenary.

This activity encourages children to ask their own questions and attempt to answer others. All views are treated with respect and considered valid. The organisation of this activity reduces adult talk and questioning and allows children to lead the topics for discussion. Like many independent activities it essential that teachers model the thought, the talk and the learning in a shared time – the emphasis is on generating debate and celebrating differences of opinion!

First impressions

Hand out a copy of a poem and read the poem aloud. Allow the children to read the poem themselves and have time for quiet thought. Ask the children to write around the poem the first impressions they have of it - using sight, sounds, and smells, making connections to their own lives, commenting on the words and their effect and so on. They may want to use Aidan Chambers' *like-dislike-puzzle-pattern* (Chambers, 2001) frame to make comments on the poem. When they have finished, their personal scribbles should surround the poem. Again, the teacher will need to model this way of interacting with a poem in a shared time before the children have a go.

Comparison Venns

This activity is another that encourages speaking and listening through debate. It asks children to 'spot the difference' and spot the similarities between poems. A Venn diagram helps to structure this. Show two poems. They should have something in common like a theme which is explored in different ways. They might look at this theme through different people, or one may rhyme and another may not and so on. 'Looking For Dad' in *Gargling with Jelly* and 'Bringing up a Single Parent' in *Juggling with Gerbils* by Brian Patten (1985, 2000) are two good examples for older children. They explore a similar theme in very different ways.

Draw a Venn diagram - two circles that overlap - effectively producing three spaces to write in. In the left and right hand space brainstorm the unique features of the two poems in terms of subject, structure, rhyme, voice, characters etc. In the middle space write down all the similarities. The discussion should highlight the speculation in readers' minds about why there are similarities and why they are differences. The use by the poet or poets of certain structures and words to create certain effects can be discussed. Again diversity of view needs to be celebrated.

Digital technologies

Many teachers are drawing on digital technologies to enhance their children's engagement with poetry. Try asking the children to produce still digital photographs that enhance a reading of the poem. Use PowerPoint™ equipment to produce a poetry presentation.

Most computers now come with video editing facilities. Ask the children to make a poetry video. Like a pop video, the moving image is used to represent the meaning of the words and rhythms within the poem. Teach the children some of the basic techniques of film making. Use the bfi and DfES (2003) guide *Look Again* to assist you. Show the children examples of pop videos to remind them of what they already know about how films make meaning. Introduce video cameras and let the children practise with them. Let them choose their locations around the school. A recital of the poem, made by the children, could be recorded as the film's sound track. Music and sound effects could also be used. Using this technology, the children's representations using the moving image become a response to the poem, producing fascinating results.

Independent poetry activities

As well as all the activities already suggested in this book, you might:

- Ask the children to illustrate poems and make 'poetry cards' for the classroom library. These consist of the poem written/word processed with the accompanying picture.
- Encourage the children to comment on poems in the class poetry books by writing their opinions on Post-it™ notes by the poems.
- Ask children to perform poetry that you give to them or they choose to use. Allow them to use theatrical props and to interpret the poem as they wish. Some poems can be used like a play script with children in groups taking the different parts. You might take digital photographs of these.
- When using narrative poems ask the children to illustrate sections of the poem for a display. Utilise different artistic media to do this.
- Ask the children to make a Word Wall (Grainger and Todd, 2000) from a poem. The children pull out words from the poem under different headings i.e. scary words, funny words, puzzling words, unusual words, unknown words and so on.
- In music lessons ask the children to compose music to accompany a poem.
- Using poems from history that have different forms of English, ask the children to speculate on the meanings of words and to 'translate' into modern English.
- Using poems from different cultures, encourage the children to read them as they think they are read within that community and again speculate on the meanings of the words.
- Ask older children to bring magazines with pop songs printed in them. Pick some of the most interesting in terms of strong themes (but appropriate for the classroom!). Share them with the class. The children will sing them to you as well as read them. Use these pop lyrics to introduce naturally the vocabulary of poetic structure and features of verse, such as rhyme patterns, chorus and stanza.
- Get the children to identify the main themes in the songs and convert them into concrete poems by re-writing the lyrics in a shape that represents the theme of the song e.g. a heart for a love song, etc.

Chapter 5

Writing poetry

The ache to utter and see in word
The silhouette of a brooding soul
    Carl Sandburg (1904, cited in Crystal and Crystal, 1941: 244)

**We come now to how teachers can encourage children to write poetry
and, more importantly, give children the motivation to want to write
poetry.** Sandburg 'ached' to write poetry; this may be a little unnecessary
and rather unwanted. Most teachers would be happy if their children 'felt'
the sensation of wanting to write it, perhaps in the same way accomplished
readers 'feel' like reading. Many of us know what it feels like to want to
pick up a book and read, but how many of us know the sensation of wanting
to write? The question is 'how to reach this point'; the point when children
have a sensation within themselves that tells them it is time to write, and
its time to write poetry? Experience tells us that this feeling will only come
when children discover what writing can do, when they feel for themselves
how writing can transform thoughts into something special.

Different Perspectives

As it seems with all aspects of English teaching, there are strong points of
view about how to encourage children to want to write poetry. In an interesting article, Anthony Wilson (2001) has usefully described three influential
perspectives. The first advocates the use of language games to introduce
children to different forms and techniques that can be found in poetry.
Sandy Brownjohn (1982, 1990) has advocated these methods. By asking
children to play with poetic devices and techniques, like metaphor and
simile, and structures like limericks or kennings, they build up a bank of
ways to manipulate words and apply them in their own writing. In her best
selling books, Brownjohn suggests ways in which children can play with
the traditional structures and forms of different kinds of poetry. As Wilson
(2001) points out, teachers can feel more secure with these methods as it

means they maintain control over decisions about 'topics, range, structure and tone of each piece' (Wilson, 2001: 5). They also have the 'advantage' (if this indeed is how it can be described) of greatly aiding the processes of monitoring, assessing and target setting in clear measurable ways.

Brownjohn's work has been very influential in the teaching of the writing of poetry in schools and has been used effectively to stimulate exciting work in many classrooms. However, this way of working has been challenged by Michael Rosen (1989). Rosen, himself, an extremely successful writer for children, sees the teaching of 'the best forms' of writing as an imposition by adults. He wants to encourage children to make their own decisions about what forms are effective for them and their own writing intentions. For Rosen, by making children write in these given forms, teachers ask children to translate their own feelings and knowledge about the world into contrived patterns of writing, ultimately dissolving the children's original creative intentions. Rosen sees form as being the choice of the writer, found from reading and discussing a range of different poets and harnessing, mixing and experimenting with those that best suit the writer's intentions. He advocates asking children to draw upon their own experiences to provide the crucial voice of their poems and to choose structures from the poems they have read in which to place them.

The third way uses examples of poems as a starting point for children's own attempts. Advocated by Jill Pirrie (1987), this strategy deliberately sets boundaries and constraints as a way to 'liberate' the creativity within the writer. Here the forms and techniques of poetry are taught explicitly using examples chosen by the teacher. As Montaigne said back in the 16th Century:

> Just as the voice of the trumpet rings out clearer and stronger for being forced through a narrow tube so too a saying leaps forth much more vigorously when compressed into the rhythms of poetry.
> (Montaigne, cited in Crystal and Crystal, 1941: 243)

For Pirrie, poets need to be conscious of their craft and work at the skills needed to perfect their abilities, only then will the benefits of working with this kind of writing show its liberating effects.

What can we learn about encouraging children to write poetry, drawing on all three stances?

1) Children will draw on the poetry they hear read to them and from what they read themselves. Research from the Centre for Literacy in Primary Education (2000) has shown that, with the help from their teachers, children draw on the texts they are exposed to and take on the techniques and styles that the authors use.

2) Children need the experiences of poetry as advocated in this book in the earlier sections to help their writing. They need to be exposed to a wide range of poetic texts.

3) In shared times these poems need to be discussed and enjoyed. Teachers will need to help children see why they enjoy the poems, by pointing out the techniques and forms that the poets employ. In some cases and for some children, this may involve the 'naming of parts' of a poem and how the poet has successfully or unsuccessfully made the meanings that s/he wanted, using these devices.

4) Children should be encouraged to draw on their own experiences to write their poems. Using their unique experiences as children will provide the subject matter of the poems and enable them to write down the thoughts, memories and feelings that have, up till then, only been lived in the mind. This helps release the voice of the child.

5) Children can be given time to choose the forms and structures they want to use from those they have been exposed to while sharing a text with teachers. Writers' workshop periods are the ideal time to do this, but some kind of independent writing time is a minimum requirement.

Tuning in to topics to write about

When children are given the opportunities to listen, read and discuss poetry they begin to understand the huge potential for self-expression it facilitates. Talking about the meanings of poems and the devices that are used to gain the powerful effects, children will want to try these for themselves.

Like famous published poets, young writers need the opportunity to write about the world, as they know it. There is still a temptation to encourage children to write on subjects traditionally linked to the works of Romantic poets - trees, flowers, snowflakes, fireworks or the pastoral landscape. Much of our best poetry comes from sensual experience and interaction with things near to us. When asking children to write poetry, teachers need to look around the environment of the school and into the world of the child. The 'stuff' of children's poems should be negotiated with them, and often will need to come from children's own interests and culture. It would be wrong to assume that we as adults can know children's interests, but we can have a go.

Michael Rosen provides a good list in his book *Did I Hear You Write* (1989), here is a few of his and mine:

- **Food**: favourites, where it's eaten and how (see Fig. 2).
- **Football**: players, games, goals, fights, and injustices.
- **Family**: loved ones, sibling arguments, worries, moving, changes, days out, days in, conversations.
- **Being bored**: the fights that result, how parents attempt to help, the reasons.
- **School**: friends, enemies, teachers, lessons, lunchtimes, playground song.
- **Fears**: dentists, injections, pain, death, schools, lessons, bullying, global war!
- **Loves**: boyfriends/girlfriends, mums, dads, pets, foods, places, games.
- **Computer games**: the games, the consoles, the friends, and the family.
- **T.V.**: the shows, the scary ones, the funny ones, the sad ones, the news reports.
- **Growing up**: changes in body, changes in feelings - all very embarrassing!
- **Possessions**: pens, pencils, soft toys, football kits, bikes, scooters, clothes.
- **Popular culture**: pop songs, pop singers, game card collections and characters, films, T.V. characters, personalities, celebrations like Christmas, Divali, Eid, Hanukkah.

The list can go on and on. Sharing opinions as a class on subjects of this nature makes their experiences, tastes and interests valid and interesting subject matter for good poems. A teacher initiating a discussion can refine the direction and content. For example, a conversation on the subject of favourite food can be worked into a discussion of where the children like to eat these foods and how. Food is a very important and personal part of children's lives and they will have much to disclose.

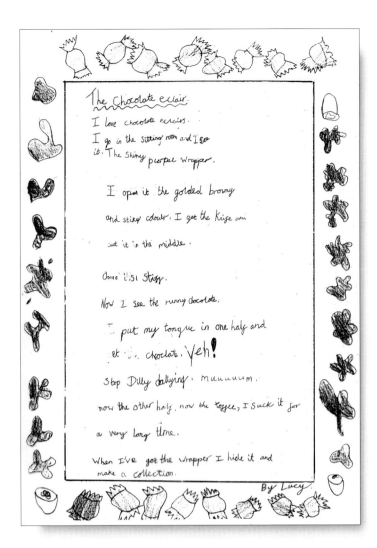

Figure 2 'The Chocolate Éclair' by Lucy

The language that children use to discuss their interests and experiences also needs to be honoured and celebrated. Poetry gives its writers licence to enrich and colour the world with non-standard English and this should be encouraged in the writing classroom!

Journals and notebooks

Give children somewhere that they can write down their first thoughts and ideas for poetry. Writing Journals are an effective way to motivate children to write independently (Graham, 1999) and they can be utilised to encourage poetry too. A writing journal is an exercise book given to each child. The journal is for private writing. The teacher agrees not to look in them unless the children give permission. Ideas for what to write are suggested and modelled by the teacher and time is given for the children to use them. This might be 15 minutes' 'early work' at the start of each day, or during independent writing times. Occasionally the teacher will ask the children to select a piece of writing from the journal that they wish to improve, ready for publication. Children will enjoy writing simple rhymes about themselves or their friends, while experimenting with simple structures and playing with language drawn from popular culture.

Jessica is the coolest
But one of the smallest
Even though she's been kissed
She's still the top of our list

Rebecca's the girl who's special
A well cool babe, it's true
She can have a laugh and a joke
And she's funky all the way through

Models

A literacy lesson provides shared time for teachers to model a range of poetry structures and techniques. Immersing children in particular kinds of poetry over set times enable children to really understand the forms modelled. These poems may be by certain poets, they may be certain kinds of poems, e.g. kennings, haiku or limericks, or they may be poems that contain poetic techniques like metaphor, alliteration or rhyming patterns. At the end of a unit of work containing poetry (see the previous section) children should try writing poetry with these specific models. However, they will need time to work on them, and this is one reason why it is essential that teachers provide time for extended writing, like a writing workshop.

Writing workshops

A writing workshop is a period for extended writing. It allows children to behave as much like an author or a poet as a school environment will allow. Children have time to work through the writing process, from composition drafts, to the editing stages and to presentation. Choices and decisions are made about the work, either on their own or in collaboration with the teacher or other children. Workshops will, in most cases, need to be at least an hour long. Many teachers in England give the last literacy lesson of the week to such a period; others find time in busy weeks in an afternoon. A regular slot is by far the best.

Workshops can:

- Allow children to work on forms of writing started during literacy lessons leading to a piece of writing to finish off a teaching unit.
- Give children the time to write a piece of their own choosing, for their own reasons. That may be poetry. Children are left to choose a form of writing, perhaps poetry with a certain structure, or using poetic techniques, that best fits their intentions and their audience. It is here that teachers can assess the success of their teaching by observing how their children approach a piece of writing and the styles and techniques they use.
- Be a time when children can write in their journals.

Workshop Structures

It always helps to tell children in advance of the workshop what you will asking them to write - a poem of their own choice on a subject of their own choice, a poem written in a certain style or structure and so on

Teachers will need to model 'how' decisions are made about what to write. Talking a writer's thoughts aloud in front of the children enables them to begin to understand the process of starting a piece of writing.

Allow children the time to talk about what they intend to write about with other children.

Writing times should be as quiet as possible. Children should not make transcription the prime concern when they are drafting. The teacher and any other adults MUST write alongside the children, this will often act as stimulation for more reluctant writers.

After writing for a short period, children should be encouraged to read their work to someone else, perhaps a designated response partner. The teacher can also show the class his/her work, sharing the doubts and/or excitements about the piece and modelling the messy beginnings of a great piece of writing!

The following weeks can be times when the work is worked on, moving towards publication. These are perfect times for the teacher to hold writing conferences with the child about the work – always respecting the editorial control the child will have over the writing. Teachers' comments can be written on 'Post-It' stickers and kept with the work. Remember that not all the writing produced in these periods will need to be converted into a publishable piece.

Displaying finished poetry

Children's poems need to be honoured by displaying them attractively. Dynamic displays of poetry will also include pictures - drawings or photographs. Allow a space for the children to comment on the finished pieces. A Post-it ™ pad enables the comments to be displayed alongside the work. These too can become rather creative and intriguing. Here is an example of a Post-it ™ note collected from Max, a year 5 Boy, by PGCE student Ian Shearer. Max understands the relationship between the work of his classmate and the world of rhyme found in popular culture - the last three verses are the chorus of a hit song. He recognises the inclusive nature of poetry and rhyme and feels free to demonstrate his understanding in this way. His pop lyric is full of the rhythms of celebration and dance and its use, as a means of responding to another poem, seems deliciously appropriate! I'm not clear who is who here.

Max is responding to a poem written by one of his peers called 'Henry the Hippy':

All the poems are hip hop to the drip drop and
Henry the Hippy is tip top and reeks of amusement!

Do ya really like it?
Do you really like it?

We're lovin' lovin' it
Lovin' it lovin' it like dis

Do you really like it?
Isn't isn't wicked!

By Max

References

Auden, W.H. and Garret, J. (1935) *The Poet's Tongue*. London: Bell

Barrs, M (2000) 'The Reader in the Writer' in *Reading* Vol.34 No.2 pp:54-60

Benton, M. (2000) 'Canons Ancient and Modern: the texts we teach'. *Educational Review*, 52: 3 November 2000 pp 269 - 277

Benton, M. & Benton, P. (1989) *Examining Poetry*. London: Hodder & Stoughton

British Film Institute and Department for Education and Skills (2003) *Look Again: A teaching guide to using film and television with three- to eleven-year olds*. London: bfi Education

Britton, J (1958) 'Reading and Writing Poetry' in G.M. Pradl *Prospect and Retrospect: Selected essays of James Britton*. Montclair: Boynton/Cook Publishers

Brown John, S. (1980) *Does it Have to Rhyme?* London: Hodder & Stoughton

Brownjohn, S. (1982) *What Rhymes with 'Secret'?* London: Hodder & Stoughton

BrownJohn, S. (1990) *The Ability to Name Cats*. London: Hodder & Stoughton

Bryant, P and Bradley, L. (1985) *Children's Reading Problems*. Oxford: Basil Blackwell

Chambers, A. (2001) *Tell Me: Children, Reading and Talk*. Stroud, Glos.: Thimble Press, 2001

Collinson, D. (1985) 'Philosophy Looks at Paintings' in E. Deighton (ed) *Looking into Paintings*. Milton Keynes: Open University

Crystal, D. (1998) *Language Play*. London: Penguin

Crystal, D. and Crystal, H. eds (1941) *Words on Words: Quotations about Language and Languages*. Middlesex: Penguin Books

Department for Education and Skills (1998) *The National Literacy Framework*. London: DfES

Department for Education and Skills (1999) *The National Curriculum for England and Wales*. London: DfES

Department for Education and Skills (2006a) *The Primary National Strategy - Literacy*. London: DfES

Department for Education and Skills (2006b) 'The New Conceptual Framework for Reading: the Simple View of Reading' - overview for literacy Leaders and managers in schools and Early Years settings'. *www.standards.dfes.gov.uk/primaryframeworks/foundation/early/simple*: accessed May 1st, 2007

Dunn, J., Styles, M. and Warburton, N. (1987) *In Tune With Yourself*. Cambridge: Cambridge University Press

Frater, G (2000) 'Observed in Practice: English in the NLS: Some Reflections' in *Reading* Vol. 34, No. 3 pp: 107-112

Goswami, U., and East, M. (2000). Rhyme and analogy in beginning reading: Conceptual and methodological issues. *Applied Psycholinguistics*, 21, 63-93.

Graham, L. (1999) 'Changing Practice Through Reflection: Key Stage 2 Reading' in *Reading* Vol. 33, No. pp: 106-113

Grainger, T, and Todd, J, (2000) *Inclusive Educational Practice: Literacy*. London: David Fulton

Jacobs, R. (2001) *A Beginner's Guide To Critical Reading: An Anthology of Literary Texts*. London: Routledge

Jefferson, A. and Robey, D. (1986) *Modern Literary Theory: A Comparative Introduction*. London: Batsford

Lambirth, A. (1997) 'Encouraging a Taste for Poetry' in M. Barrs and M. Rosen eds *A Year With Poetry*. London: Centre for Language in Primary Education

National Reading Panel (2000) *Teaching Children to Read*. Washington DC: NIH Publications

Patten, B. (1985) *Gargling With Jelly*. London: Puffin

Patten, B. (2000) *Juggling With Gerbils*. London: Puffin

Pirrie, J. (1987) *On Common Ground: A Programme for Teaching Poetry*. Sevenoaks: Hodder & Stoughton

Rose, J. (2006) *Independent Review of the Teaching of Early Reading: Final Report*. Nottingham: DfES

Rosen, M. (1989) *Did I Hear You Write?* Nottingham: Five Leaves

Rosen, M. (ed) (1985) *The Kingfisher Book of Children's Poetry*. London: Kingfisher

Scannell, V. (1987) *How To Enjoy Poetry*. London: Piatkus

Victorian Curriculum and Assessment Authority (VCAA) (2004) *Victorian Curriculum Reform 2004: Consultation Paper*. East Melbourne: VCAA

Wilson, A. (2001) 'Brownjohn, Hughes, Pirrie and Rosen: What Rhymes with Oral Writing?' in *English in Education* Vol. 35, No. 2, pp: 3 - 11

Zephaniah, B. (1997) *School's Out: Poems Not For School*. Edinburgh: AK Press